Light Up Your World

Empowering High School Girls to Dare to Shine

Sonya D. Nelson

Light Up Your World: Empowering High School Girls to Dare to Shine
Copyright © 2023 by Sonya D. Nelson

All rights reserved. No part of this book may be reproduced or transmitted in any form or by any means without written permission from the author.

ISBN 9798852190703

Dedication

To each, and every, high school girl who holds this book in her hands, know that you are capable of greatness. Embrace your authenticity, spread kindness, dream big, laugh often, and cast fear aside. The world awaits your brilliance, and I have unwavering faith in your ability to change it for the better.

Contents

Dedication 6
Introduction 10
Finding Confidence in Being Yourself 13
Doing Good for Yourself and Others 24
Seizing the Day and Nurturing Your Aspirations......... 33
Laughing Your Way to Resilience............................. 44
Overcoming Fear and Taking Bold Steps 56

Matthew 5:14-16

New International Version (NIV)

"You are the light of the world. A town built on a hill cannot be hidden. Neither do people light a lamp and put it under a bowl. Instead they put it on its stand, and it gives light to everyone in the house. In the same way, let your light shine before others, that they may see your good deeds and glorify your Father in heaven."

Introduction

In a world filled with endless possibilities, the journey of a high school girl is a remarkable tapestry of dreams, aspirations, challenges, and triumphs. It is a time of self-discovery, growth, and transformation—a pivotal period that lays the foundation for the incredible individuals you are destined to become. It is within this context that this book, "Light Up Your World: Empowering High School Girls," takes shape.

From the moment I set out to write this book, my heart was filled with an unwavering belief in the extraordinary potential of high school girls. I have witnessed firsthand the resilience, creativity, and sheer brilliance that emanates from each one of you. This book was written to empower you to embrace your uniqueness, develop your strengths, and overcome any obstacles that stand in your way.

My wish is that the words on the following pages ignite the fire within you. I want to remind you that no dream is too big, no obstacle insurmountable, and no goal beyond your reach. It celebrates your authenticity, your dreams, your laughter, and your unwavering spirit. It acknowledges the challenges you face and provides tools and strategies to navigate them with grace and resilience.

"Light Up Your World" is a call to action—a rallying cry for you to step into your power, embrace your passions, and make a positive impact on the world. It recognizes that empowerment is not a solitary pursuit but a collective movement. Together, we can create a world where every high school girl feels seen, heard, and valued.

As you embark on this transformative journey, remember that you are not alone. You are part of a vibrant community of high school girls who are blazing trails, challenging norms, and reshaping the world. Seek support, lean on one another, and celebrate each other's successes. Together, we are a force to be reckoned with.

So, my dear high school girls, let this book be your guiding light, your companion, and your source of inspiration. Let it remind you that you have the power to illuminate your world and the world around you. Embrace your authenticity, dream big, unleash your laughter, and cast aside fear. It is time to shine brightly, for you are destined for greatness.

Here's to boundless hope and unwavering belief in your potential...

Chapter One

Finding Confidence in Being Yourself

As a young adult, I know that this isn't an easy question to answer because you are surrounded by a lot of people who are telling you what to and what not to do. And let's be honest, you care more about what your friends think. Who you are and what you're worth is tied up in what *they* think and say about you.

Consider the number of times you may have been talking to a friend, and you talked about everything and everybody but YOU? How many times have people's response been, "Girl! I know about all that, but I want to talk about YOU! What's goin' on with you these days?" You nervously laugh and search your mind for a way to change the subject. You do that because you know that the thought you have isn't worth mentioning.

You've forgotten that you are meant to be different...

You aren't meant to look, be, or act like anyone else...

Who are YOU? What version of YOU is screaming to be seen? To be heard?

Too often we try to fix ourselves up so that friends or family members will be comfortable, but we are dying inside. Take time out to discover your authentic self. Standing out doesn't have to be viewed as a weakness.

Who ELSE are you listening to? You can't let everyone give you advice on things because they might have a hidden motive you may not know about.

Let me explain what I mean...

The guy you like keeps telling you that you need to lose weight. You trust what he says because you believe he likes you, right? He mentions it all day, every day, and you start to listen because you want him to be happy with you. But have you ever looked at yourself and said, "You know what? I'm not overweight at all! So why does he keep saying that all the time?" Then you figure it out—you're getting too much attention. Therefore, he finds something "wrong" with you that he knows you will pay attention to if he mentions it enough. He wants you to be self-conscious, wondering if he is going to continue to date you if you don't lose weight. This becomes a double-edged sword because, if you do lose weight, he just might come back and say that you've lost TOO much, setting you off once again.

Perhaps it's the friend that you work with after school or take classes with that does not want you to quit that job or study extra hard to make good grades. They will talk you out of doing things that allow you to better yourself. These 'friends' will prey on your feelings by telling you that they will be lonely or that you do not have to study so much because high school should be fun.

Pretty soon, you will start to second guess your decisions, not seeing that these friends do not want anything different for themselves. They want you to be miserable with them because they do not want to do the work to have a better situation at work or at school. You side with your BEST friend. You decided to listen and unfortunately you have become just as miserable as they are. You've now conformed to what everyone else wanted and your path to joy, happiness, or even peace becomes tucked away once again.

Or it can be that friend who is ALWAYS talking down about your goals and what you want to do. You can tell them that you got an A on a project, and they will tell you that it doesn't count because that teacher is known for doing this or that with their students' grades.

The bad part about this is that the people who are saying and doing this stuff to us are our closest friends. You wonder if they are trying to block you from being what you want to be and what God wants you to be. You find that you can't talk to them anymore about anything that you want to do or want in life. You go quiet because now you are more worried about their opinion of you and what you want to do.

Whose voice are you listening to—theirs or God's? There is a big difference. You may not understand that right now, but there is. How do you know? Someone who is speaking to you with God's voice is going to remind you that He created you in HIS image, which means that you ARE indeed SPECIAL! They will tell you that your life is about the decisions that YOU make for YOURSELF and not for others because, when someone asks you why you did something, they aren't going to want to hear about other people... Don't get caught up in their mess!

YOU ARE VALUABLE NO MATTER WHAT THEY SAY TO OR ABOUT YOU—remember that! Let me tell you what my friend Tammie told me—what YOU show to the world everyday MATTERS! So, with that in mind, SHOW UP AND SHINE!

Have you ever heard someone say that you have to teach people how to treat you? That means that people will treat you according to the way you respond to what they do. When you don't speak up for yourself and fight back against someone who is mistreating you, that means that you are allowing them to take down your value. You want to keep that person around, so you become less than what you were so they will be happy with you. NO ONE IS WORTH THAT!

What you ALLOW will CONTINUE!

Let people know where the line is and protect that line, baby girl! You don't have to be flamboyant or rude, but people need to know how far they can go. If you don't, you'll end up constantly feeling hurt, ashamed, and weak—none of which you HAVE to EVER be in LIFE!

When you allow other people to determine how much you are worth, you become invisible. They will feel like they can speak for you, volunteer you to do things, and more because you have let them make you invisible.

Think about the time when you had a great idea, and your friend stole it and passed it off as their own. When you checked them about it, they said that you were lying and not smart enough to come up with something like that. Then, once no one else is around, they will apologize and beg you not to tell anyone that it wasn't their idea. They promise that they won't do it again and that they REALLY need this good grade or chance at something. You'll just nod your head and let it go.

When you let it go, you will start to make their situation yours. You'll start doing work and other things for them because your mind keeps telling you that they need that good grade or chance at something. Soon, your grades are slipping, and your work is going undone. You won't even notice until you get into trouble. Then, this same friend will keep coming to you because they see how much time and effort you used to help them. The fact that you're failing doesn't mean anything to them at all. If they are passing, nothing else matters.

If someone else tries to help, they will say they don't need them because they have you and you won't know anything about what they told someone else you are going to do. When you find out, they will move heaven and earth trying to make you think that you are the only person who could help them. They will know that they're wrong and they will say what they think you want to hear so you won't be mad at them anymore. Baby girl, PAY ATTENTION!

When you do, you'll start to see through everything they're doing and saying. You'll see that you have made excuses for them that you didn't need to make. You'll tell yourself that they didn't mean what they said or did, but you know that they did!

Don't allow them to make you forget who YOU are and what YOU want to do.

You don't owe them anything, no matter what they did for you in the past.

Their peace isn't worth yours.

They don't always know what's best for YOU!

Their position in your life doesn't make them right.

Build a relationship with God and let HIM show you who you are meant to be—that's what matters more than anything.

The first step in showing up and shining is to reclaim your self-worth and remember who YOU are.

Unleash Your S.H.I.N.E.

Shake what others have tried to make you out to be.

Heal yourself by embracing who you are.

Invite God into your space to inspire and ignite your creativity.

Notice what true colors others are showing you.

Encourage yourself to go after your hopes and dreams!

Self-Reflections for Shining: Illuminate Your Inner Self

1. Whose voice am I listening to?

   _____
   _____
   _____
   _____
   _____
   _____
   _____

2. Do I believe I am enough and worthy of what I want? If not, why?

   _____
   _____
   _____
   _____
   _____
   _____

3. Do I know how valuable I am?

4. Why am I allowing others to dictate who I am?

5. How does that make me feel? If the answer is negative, why I am letting people make me feel this way?

Chapter Two

Doing Good for Yourself and Others

My aspiration to help people began at an early age. Around the age of twelve I began volunteering with my church's youth group. From group homes to nursing homes, the experiences were truly invaluable for me. Unable to wrap my head around it, I just knew that it was deeper than me. I felt accomplished. I felt purposeful. Exhibiting small acts of kindness to others put life in perspective for me. You learn about yourself and how to have empathy for others. From this point on, the spark was there.

What can I say, doing good just feels good.

Doing good is a goal that every one of us should have. Many young adults are selfish today and not in a good way. There is a good type of selfishness and a bad type of selfishness.

The good type of selfishness is when you take the time that you use doing for everyone else and instead doing something for yourself. You're important, too.

The bad type of selfishness is when you are so wrapped up in your own life that you can't see the needs of others with which you can help.

When you see that someone has a need that you can do something about and you don't help, that's not a good look for you. This is especially so when the person in need and the people around y'all know that you can help. That will come back on you—just wait!

When you *intentionally* ignore someone who needs help, that's selfishness.

When you can't share a positive word with someone who is having a bad day, that's selfishness.

When someone comes to you to talk about what they're going through and you make the conversation all about you, that is selfish!

When you say, "Well, I don't have….", you aren't always telling the truth. The truth is that you want to use the money for something that you're going to eat, break or grow out of instead of helping that person who has a life altering need.

Let's break this down even more. The need doesn't always have to be related to money. It could be giving someone something to eat when they're hungry. Giving a ride to someone because their car broke down. (And even in this instance, be extremely cautious. This is not to say that everyone you see stranded on the side of the road, you should pull over and offer a ride to.) It could also be as simple as offering a pencil or a sheet of notebook paper to a classmate because they don't have it.

Not seeing the needs of others can make our lives worse!

You'll start to wonder why nothing is going right for you and then you're reminded of that person you could have helped but you didn't.

Now you have the same problem that they do and need help, yet you can't get it.

Now the people YOU are calling for help are brushing you off, not reading or responding to your texts, and not answering your calls.

What you may fail to realize is that it took everything in that person to *not* ask you for help. Do you not recognize how some people don't want to be a bother to others? Or that they may even feel ashamed for having to ask? Is it silly of them to think that just for once you would stop thinking about yourself long enough to help them?

Blessings come from doing for others when it's in our power to do so.

It doesn't have to be anything big, either.

Think about how happy you are when you find out that someone you know is watching the same shows as you. You are beyond excited because now you have someone to talk shop with when you may not have had that before.

This is a staple within my family. We often watch the same shows on our favorite day of the week and compare notes. More times than not I end up on the phone with my sisters or my mom watching it together, screaming or laughing at the antics of the show's cast.

My children and I also have a set of shows or movies we watch together. My husband and I share an interest in certain programs as well. For me, it's like our special bonding time. Something THIS small can make a world of difference in someone's life. It makes a difference in my life for sure.

How can something that you enjoy doing be a blessing to someone else? I encourage you to find someone to help with those hobbies and interests you have. There just might be someone watching who will secretly bless you for it.... You never know!

I want to challenge you to do one more thing—don't sound off about what you did for someone. For example, you're among your friends, and you decide that you're going to let someone have it today. Your day started off on the wrong foot; therefore, you're going to return the favor to an unsuspecting peer.

The peer is not your bestie, but you're cool with one another. And you have helped one another several times before. She walks by you in the hallway at school and you start going on about how you did "this, that, and the other" for her. You feel like you need to announce it to all the surrounding students, now a problem ensues. Other peers are joking and making inappropriate comments. The person is embarrassed and caught off guard by the behavior.

What you do for others isn't always meant to be known and there are reasons for that.

First, the person you helped may not want others to know they had that need.

Second, doing so might cause the person to feel they can't trust you with their needs anymore.

Third, the person you helped now feels compelled to pay you back when that isn't even the case. They will do it because they don't want you to see them as a burden in any way. Before you get mad about that, see things from their side. Had you not said anything, this wouldn't even have happened! It's not THEIR fault you're mad.

Lastly, the people you're trying to impress may not even pay what you did any attention. Also, they'll wonder why you even did it if you're going to blast it everywhere. They will shake their heads, laugh, and roll their eyes because they already know what the aftermath will be.

Even if they are impressed, your attitude about the whole thing will not sit well with them. They will start watching you for the wrong reasons.

If you are looking to do good, why?

Why do you want to help?

Is it so you can say that you did something to help someone?

Are you being nice to them to get back at them for being mean to you?

It's important that we check our motives behind what we are about to do. People know when you're not being genuine with them, and they take note of that. You can't fool everybody all the time. So, while you hope that no one sees your true motives, know that someone does. However, they won't tell YOU that!

There is too much good to be done in the world for it to be done for the wrong reasons!

The person you help may never be able to repay you but know that life has a great way of rewarding the right motives!

Unleash Your S.H.I.N.E.

Shake what others have tried to make you out to be.

Heal yourself by embracing who you are.

Invite God into your space to inspire and ignite your creativity.

Notice what true colors others are showing you.

Encourage yourself to go after your hopes and dreams!

Self-Reflections for Shining: Illuminate Your Inner Self

1. How do I define "doing good" to myself and others?

   _____
   _____
   _____
   _____
   _____
   _____
   _____
   _____
   _____

2. What are my hobbies and interests? (Reflect on your strengths, skills, and talents.)

   _____
   _____
   _____

_____
_____
_____
_____
_____

3. How can I use my hobbies and interests to make a positive impact on others?

_____
_____
_____
_____
_____
_____
_____

4. What values and principles are important to me? Are my actions aligned with those values?

_____
_____
_____
_____
_____
_____
_____

Chapter Three

Seizing the Day and Nurturing Your Aspirations

There is a time and place for everything, but I know how it is to be your age. You want what you want, and you want it now, no matter what the result will be.

You hate it when someone tells you to wait or that you're wasting your time. Yet, for you to live your best life, there are things you will have to start doing. There are things you will have to stop doing. You don't have to struggle with procrastination or fear of failure.

High school is a transformative period in every young person's life, full of opportunities and potential for growth. For high school girls, it is crucial to embrace this phase with determination and seize the day. Embracing your strengths, fostering positive relationships, and setting ambitious goals, are just a few steps you can use to unlock your full potential and create a promising future.

Let's talk about your individual strengths. One of the first steps to seizing the day is to recognize and embrace your strengths. Each of us possesses unique talents, skills, and qualities that contribute to our personal growth and success.

Really? You may ask. YES, REALLY! Looking into your strengths may not be at the top of to-do list, but it is key to finding out your passion and building your self-confidence early. Don't get me wrong, this process can be challenging to find those strengths within ourselves. Often, we take our strengths for granted or recognize that thing that we're really good at as being a "strength."

Consider the different hobbies or activities you engage in. Some of those activities may be natural gifts for you. Do you have an interest in singing, photography, writing, drama, sports, or art? Pay attention to the things that you enjoy doing. And if you're saying you don't know what you like, then I encourage you to step out of your comfort zone and allow you to discover those hidden talents and skill sets.

Feedback from others is also good in discovering your strengths. However, let me insert a disclaimer here: YOU HAVE TO BE OPEN TO CONSTRUCTIVE CRITICISM! Baby, when I say you may need a lot of prayer and thick skin... It can be difficult to hear different perspectives because as you are discovering talents, you are also learning to embrace them and the weaknesses in those talents. We're not perfect and all have areas we need to improve upon.

Remember, girls, we all have unique strengths and talents. Embrace them, nurture them, and let them shine!!

A strong support system is vital for any high school girl aiming to seize the day. Building positive relationships with friends, teachers, mentors, and family members creates an environment of encouragement and inspiration. Take a moment and think about who you surround yourself with. Is your circle one of like-minded individuals who uplift and motivate or are they the mean girls who cause and stir up drama?

Positive relationships can provide guidance, advice, and emotional support, fostering a sense of belonging and empowerment. High school girls need a supportive network that can assist them in making a positive impact not only in their personal lives but also within their peers and community. Negative relationships may cause you to take a closer look at yourself, your values, your boundaries (or lack of), leaving you unfulfilled. Yet, the lessons learned through experiencing unhealthy patterns could very well be the catalyst to cause you to seek out healthier connections.

Lastly, you must set some goals for the day. What is the most important thing you need to get done for the day? I mean that thing that should get done even if you do nothing else that day. Once you know that, focus on making it happen.

Before I go any further with goals, let me explain. Have you ever heard of S.M.A.R.T. goals? SMART is an acronym that stands for Specific, Measurable, Achievable, Relevant, and Time-bound. It is an outline used to help you create clear and actionable goals.

Let's break down each component of SMART goals:

Specific: A goal should be well-defined and specific. It should answer the questions of who, what, where, when, and why. For example, instead of saying "I want to improve my grades," you could say, "I want improve my overall GPA from a 3.0 to a 3.3 by the end of the first semester."

Measurable: Goals should be measurable so that you can track your progress and determine when you have achieved them. Using the previous example, the goal of improving your GPA is measurable because you can track your progress by calculating your average at the end of each grading period.

Achievable: A goal should be realistic and attainable. It should be challenging but not so overwhelming that it becomes unattainable. For example, dedicating additional study time, attending classes every day, and turning in assignments on time is attainable. Setting an unrealistic goal may lead to frustration and disappointment.

Relevant: Goals should be relevant and support your overall objectives and values. They should be meaningful to you and contribute to your personal or professional growth. Using the previous example, improving your grades is important because it can enhance your academic opportunities.

Time-bound: Goals should have a specific time frame or deadline for completion. Setting a deadline creates a sense of urgency and helps you stay focused and accountable. In our example, you can achieve this goal within the next three to four months, by the end of your first semester.

When it comes to your goals, look at what's motivating you to achieve that goal. Is it something you really want to do or are you using that to hide what your real intentions are? Honey, there is NO time for that. Let me explain why...

If you have the wrong reasons for goals, you will find yourself doing things that you shouldn't be to get them done. You won't even care if you hurt someone else as long as you get what you want. Then, when you see that they are really hurt, now you can't be around them. What you did is going to bother you so much that you'll see that what you wanted wasn't all that.

If you have the right reasons for your goals, you will help somebody else when you get them done. Someone needs to know that reaching that goal can be done. There are people rooting for you, so getting things done lets them know they didn't waste time, money, or effort on you. More opportunities will come for you because people will see that you are about your business.

Aside from having your goals in check, watch how you spend your time. If there are things that need to be done before you go to school or right when you get home, you don't need to be on the phone with that one friend you can talk to forever! Why? It's because you'll end up running late and get in trouble for not having things done.

If you wrote down how you spent every hour of your day, would you be happy about what you did? I did this for one day and I didn't like what I saw at all. I spent a lot of time doing things that weren't important.

Instead of getting mad about what you see, do better! Ask yourself how you can use your time more wisely.

You don't have to take that phone call.

You don't have to answer that text message right now.

You don't have to go down the rabbit hole of social media.

You may also start to notice that you spend a lot of time doing things that you could have done later. How many times have you thought about what you could have been doing   instead of what you did?

This is one of the reasons why the adults in your life are always on you about what you do with your time. They fuss at you about playing games or being on the phone instead of doing your homework. Then you get mad because you need help, and they tell you to figure it out on your own. Now, you're up all night trying to get it done – or not. The next morning, they say something like, "Uh huh! I bet you won't play games all day no more!" You roll your eyes even though you know they're right.

Do you check yourself that way or do you assume that you know what you're doing? You know that you could have finished your homework in an hour, but you chose to be on the phone.

Do you wait to do things until the last minute? Now, when it's time to make moves, you can't because you're not ready.

Do you get mad at your friends when you see that they have things done? You are so jealous of them because they took the time to do what was necessary. It's not them you're mad at, though. They don't have extra help or a secret sauce—they simply put their work first.

Take consistent action and you can achieve remarkable things.

Unleash Your S.H.I.N.E.

Shake what others have tried to make you out to be.

Heal yourself by embracing who you are.

Invite God into your space to inspire and ignite your creativity.

Notice what true colors others are showing you.

Encourage yourself to go after your hopes and dreams!

Self-Reflections for Shining: Illuminate Your Inner Self

1. What does seizing the day mean to me personally?

   _____
   _____
   _____
   _____
   _____
   _____
   _____
   _____

2. How do I feel when I step outside of my comfort zone to try something new?

   _____
   _____
   _____
   _____

_____
_____
_____
_____

3. What habits or activities drain my energy or hold me back from seizing the day? What changes can I make?

_____
_____
_____
_____
_____
_____
_____

4. Who inspires or motivates me to live my life to the fullest?

_____
_____
_____
_____
_____
_____

Chapter Four

Laughing Your Way to Resilience

Have you ever heard that laughter is medicine for the soul? Laughter can have a positive impact on your overall well-being. There is a therapeutic effect that can bring comfort, strength, joy, and even peace into your life.

I'm not a doctor, and I can't explain the science behind it. I just know there is a "power" laughter has - to heal, uplift spirits and strengthen relationships.

Let's examine further.

Has anyone ever attempted to make you laugh when you were mad? How did you feel? Did you continue to stay angry? Or did you embrace the moment of laughter? Your friends made you laugh because they didn't want you to be mad anymore.

Laughter is like a secret superpower we have. It brings us together and makes everything more enjoyable. When we laugh together, it creates a bond among us. It breaks down barriers and makes us feel connected. It's such a great feeling to share laughter with friends.

And do you know what else? Laughter is also good for our mental health. It's like a natural stress reliever. Whenever I'm feeling overwhelmed, a good laugh can instantly lift my spirits. Consider those tough exam weeks, laughter is like a breath of fresh air. It releases those feel-good hormones that make you feel happier and more relaxed. It's like a mini mental vacation.

But laughter does more than just improve our mood. It builds our confidence too. When we laugh, we feel more comfortable and freer. It's like all our worries disappear, and we can be ourselves without any inhibitions. It's that moment of liberation when we're laughing so hard that we don't care what others think. It enhances our self-esteem and helps us embrace our unique qualities. It's like a confidence booster.

Laughter is like a language of its own. Through shared laughter, we develop empathy and improve our social skills. It makes conversations flow more naturally, and it's so much   easier to express ourselves.

Laughter creates a positive learning environment too. When we laugh during classes or group activities, it lightens the mood and makes learning more enjoyable. It's like we're more engaged and motivated to learn.

When we laugh while studying or discussing topics, it's easier to remember things. It's like laughter activates our brain and helps us retain information. Learning becomes a fun experience – even in high school. High school can be a more vibrant and enjoyable journey. It's not just about the academic side; it's about creating memories, forging friendships, and embracing the joy of laughter.

Laughing is also a lot like crying. They have a lot more in common than we might think, especially when it comes to high school girls. You may be wondering, 'How so? They seem like such opposite emotions.' That's true but think about it. Both laughter and crying are forms of emotional release. When we laugh, it's often because something funny or joyful has touched us deeply. And when we cry, it's usually because we're feeling sad or overwhelmed. They're both expressions of our emotions, just in different ways.

And just like crying, laughter can be liberating. It allows us to let go of pent-up emotions and release stress. Sometimes, when we've had a tough day, a good laugh can be just as therapeutic as shedding a few tears. Laughter can be a way for us to process our emotions, like crying. They serve as outlets for our emotions. They help us acknowledge and express how we feel, even if it's in different ways. It's like they're two sides of the same coin.

They both remind us that we're human, with a wide range of emotions. And as high school girls navigating the complexities of adolescence, it's important for you to embrace and acknowledge your emotions, whether through laughter or tears.

It's important for you to honor and appreciate those moments, whether they make us laugh or cry. So, let's remember that laughter and crying are more alike than they may seem. They both allow you to express yourselves authentically and help you to navigate the rollercoaster of emotions that come with being a high school girl.

When you laugh, you make other people around you laugh, even if they don't know what you're laughing about! It also makes you change the way you think about things. You start to see what's going right around you and see the good things.

When I think about my time in high school, I tend to smile and laugh a lot. There are so many different episodes of silliness that I either participated in or witnessed. Imagine a scenario where a group of girls is attempting to reenact a popular dance routine during band rehearsal. Everything goes horribly wrong, fast. Yet, despite our, I mean 'their' lack of coordination, we all end up in belly aching fits of laughter.

Perhaps you're in the school cafeteria, and the day has been going well. It's just time to sit, eat, and chill with your friends for a little social commentary. But as you are walking past a table, where your crush just happens to be sitting, you accidentally spill something on him. When he says, "It's all good.", instead of feeling embarrassed, you both burst into laughter, diffusing the tension, and turning an awkward moment into a lighthearted memory.

In high school, experimenting with fashion is also common, and sometimes girls end up with unexpected outfits. For instance, your friend might accidentally wear mismatched socks. She is unaware of her fashion faux pas until her friends point it out during a class presentation. The entire class bursts in laughter, including the girl herself, turning her fashion mishap into a memorable and amusing moment.

High school is full of surprises, and unexpected reactions can lead to laughter. Your high school journey is one where you can, and should, create cherished memories that will be remembered long after you have left. The stories of laughter that kept spirits high and added excitement to your high school experience.

Let's slightly turn the tables here and provide another perspective of laughing.

Is there a downside to laughing? There is…

While laughter is generally a positive and enjoyable experience, there can be situations in high school where laughter may not be appropriate or may have negative consequences. Here are a few scenarios when laughter may not be a good thing with high school girls:

* Bullying or Mocking: Laughing at someone's expense, particularly when it involves bullying or mocking, is hurtful and can have long-lasting negative effects. If a group of girls laughs at a classmate's appearance, abilities, or personal struggles, it creates a toxic and harmful environment that can lead to emotional distress and damaged self-esteem.

* Insensitive Jokes or Comments: High school can be a time when girls are navigating their identities and facing various challenges. Laughing at jokes or making insensitive comments about sensitive topics such as race, body image, mental health, or personal tragedies can be hurtful and contribute to a culture of exclusion and discrimination.

* Embarrassing or Humiliating Others: There may be instances where a girl unintentionally embarrasses or humiliates someone through pranks or practical jokes. While harmless pranks can be fun, it's essential to consider the feelings and boundaries of others. Laughing at someone's expense without their consent can create a negative atmosphere and strain relationships.

* Dismissing Serious Situations: There are times when serious situations arise in high school, such as conflicts, accidents, or personal crises. In these moments, laughter can be seen as dismissive or insensitive. Laughing when someone is genuinely upset or distressed can make them feel invalidated and unsupported, hindering the formation of trust and empathy.

Insert yourself in any of the above-mentioned scenarios. How would you feel? Or maybe you have already experienced being bullied or humiliated. Think about it. You probably didn't find anything humorous in it. I can recall a few times in high school where I overheard some people talking about me that I thought were friends. The things that were said really hurt; however, I never confronted them. Even to this day, they don't even know I heard them. What it did for me was change the trajectory of the type of friends I wanted to have. I became freer when I surrounded myself with friends who showed they cared, who made me laugh, who genuinely supported ME.

Laughter in high school, particularly among girls, plays a crucial role in building connections, reducing stress, boosting confidence, enhancing creativity, and promoting mental well-being. It's important to be mindful of the impact our laughter can have on others and to treat each other with empathy, respect, and kindness; especially, when it's in our power to do so.

Unleash Your S.H.I.N.E.

Shake what others have tried to make you out to be.

Heal yourself by embracing who you are.

Invite God into your space to inspire and ignite your creativity.

Notice what true colors others are showing you.

Encourage yourself to go after your hopes and dreams!

Self-Reflections for Shining: Illuminate Your Inner Self

1. How does laughter positively impact my overall well-being and mental health?

   _____
   _____
   _____
   _____
   _____
   _____
   _____
   _____

2. In what ways does laughter help to relieve stress and improve my mood?

   _____
   _____
   _____

_____
_____
_____
_____
_____

3. Can laughter strengthen my relationships with friends and family? How?

_____
_____
_____
_____
_____
_____
_____
_____

4. Am I able to laugh at myself and find humor in my own mistakes or shortcomings? Why or why not?

_____
_____
_____
_____
_____
_____
_____
_____

5. Do I actively seek out opportunities for laughter, such as watching comedy shows, sharing funny

stories, or engaging in playful activities?

_____
_____
_____
_____
_____
_____
_____

6. What steps can I take to incorporate more laughter into my daily life and encourage others to do the same?

_____
_____
_____
_____
_____
_____
_____
_____

Chapter Five

Overcoming Fear and Taking Bold Steps

In Marianne Williamson's book "A Return to Love: Reflections on the Principles of A Course in Miracles," lies a poem called "Our Deepest Fear." There are some profound lessons within this inspirational piece that can help guide us towards a path of embracing our potential and overcoming our fears. I feel this poem resonates with the very essence of your journey of self-discovery and personal growth, urging you to drop the limitations that hold you back and step into your authentic power. Through Williamson's insightful words, we are all reminded that our fears are not who we are and that by confronting and embracing them, we can unleash our unlimited potential.

Let's explore the reflective insight of "Our Deepest Fear" and embark on a transformative journey of self-empowerment and growth together.

"Our Deepest Fear"

"Our deepest fear is not that we are inadequate.

Our deepest fear is that we are powerful beyond measure.

It is our light, not our darkness, that most frightens us.

We ask ourselves, 'who am I to be brilliant, gorgeous, talented, fabulous?'

Actually, who are you not to be?

You are a child of God. Your playing small does not serve the World.

There is nothing enlightening about shrinking

so that other people won't feel insecure around you.

We were born to make manifest the glory of God that is within us.

It is not just in some of us; it is in everyone.

As we let our own light shine,

we consciously give other people permission to do the same.

As we are liberated from our own fear,

our presence automatically liberates others."

Take a minute to read that poem again.

What is YOUR deepest fear? What does it stop you from doing? Fear is a universal emotion experienced by individuals of all ages, and high school girls are no exception. While fear can serve as a protective mechanism, alerting individuals to potential dangers, it can also have profound effects on our lives and especially among young girls. Fear influences our thoughts, actions, and overall well-being.

Using the poem as our guide, I believe that "Our Deepest Fear" provides valuable insights and practical strategies that empower you to face and overcome your fears. Because high school girls often experience a wide range of fears, some of which can be healthy and protective, while others can be unhealthy and limiting, we'll examine a few scenarios that may offer a deeper understanding.

Let's talk about how exploring self-reflection, embracing vulnerability, seeking support, fostering resilience and visualization, can develop the tools necessary to navigate your fears and awaken unexplored talents. To overcome our deepest fears, you and I must embark on a journey of self-reflection and embrace our authenticity. Ask yourself: What are my fears? Are the fears rooted in external judgments or internal insecurities? By understanding the origins of our fears, we can gain clarity and perspective, enabling ourselves to challenge limiting beliefs and embrace our true selves. Your worth extends far beyond what others think of you.

The poem reminds us that our playing small does not serve the world. You must recognize that growth often lies on the other side of fear. Step outside of your comfort zones, take risks, and embrace vulnerability. Try new experiences, whether it be joining a club, trying out for a sports team, or speaking up in class. You can build confidence and resilience. Mistakes and failures are part of the learning process, and each setback is an opportunity for growth.

No journey to overcome fears is meant to be traveled alone. You should seek guidance and support from trusted individuals, such as parents, teachers, mentors, or friends. These individuals can offer valuable insights, advice, and reassurance. Additionally, these support systems can provide encouragement and accountability, reminding you of your strengths and supporting them throughout your journey of overcoming fears.

Resilience, or strength, is a vital attribute when facing and overcoming fears. I encourage you to view setbacks as temporary obstacles rather than impossible hurdles. Adopt a growth mindset by reminding yourself that challenges provide opportunities for growth and learning. You can develop resilience by learning coping strategies, such as positive self-talk and stress management techniques. View fear as a steppingstone towards personal development and inner strength.

Visualizing success and affirming positive beliefs can be powerful tools for overcoming fears. Visualize yourself successfully navigating your fears and achieving your goals. Through positive affirmations, you can reframe your thoughts and cultivate a mindset that supports growth and success. The mind is a powerful tool, and by utilizing its potential, it can manifest your desires and conquer your deepest fears.

When you focus on your fear, you get stuck. I've been there and I've definitely done that. Fear has kept me "stuck" for a significant amount of time. I've also had to have people push me from fear's hamster wheel a time or two. Honestly, some days, I'm still there. I haven't arrived. I'm ever evolving.

Fear can cause you to be too scared to do anything and it's like your fear has you in jail. You think that something is going to go wrong if you try anything. You feel like you will disappoint your friends and family if you do anything. What is that fear and how long will you let it bother you?

Let's visit a few scenarios about the healthy and unhealthy side of fear.

Scenario 1: Healthy Side of Fear

Phoebe is approached by her teacher to participate in a public speaking competition. She feels a flood of fear and anxiety about speaking in front of a large audience. However, Phoebe recognizes that this fear is a natural response and a chance for personal growth. She decides to embrace the opportunity, seeking guidance from her teacher and practicing her speech diligently. Phoebe acknowledges that her fear is pushing her to prepare thoroughly, resulting in a well-rehearsed presentation. On the day of the competition, she experiences butterflies in her stomach but manages to deliver a confident and inspiring speech, impressing both the judges and her peers. Through facing her fear head-on, Phoebe not only conquers the challenge but also gains self-assurance and a sense of accomplishment.

Scenario 2: Unhealthy Side of Fear

Ziva dreams of pursuing a career in art. However, she is constantly terrified by the fear of failure and rejection. Ziva believes that her artwork will never be good enough and worries excessively about what others might think. Her fear paralyzes her, preventing her from sharing her work with others or seeking constructive criticism. Ziva's fear becomes a hindrance to her growth and development as an artist. She compares herself to others and feels discouraged when she perceives their work to be better. Her fear traps her in a cycle of self-doubt, leading to missed opportunities and limited progress. To overcome this unhealthy side of fear, Ziva needs to recognize that making mistakes and receiving feedback are vital to the creative process. She should seek support from mentors to gain confidence and push through her fear, allowing her artistic abilities to flourish.

Scenario 3: Healthy Side of Fear

Gia is passionate about pursuing a career in medicine. Science is her favorite subject. She applies for a competitive summer internship at a local hospital that was opening to high school seniors. Upon receiving an interview invitation, Gia feels a mixture of excitement and fear. She is very aware of the significance of the opportunity and the potential challenges she may face. Yet, she uses this fear as a driving force to prepare thoroughly. She researches common interview questions, practices her responses, and seeks advice from others. During the interview, Gia's fear shows up in the form of focus and determination, helping her present herself confidently and articulate her goals effectively. Gia's fear pushes her to perform her best, and she ultimately gets the internship, gaining valuable experience in the medical field.

Scenario 4: Unhealthy Side of Fear

Zuri has always wanted to join the school's soccer team. However, she embraces a deep fear of failure and rejection. Zuri constantly doubts her abilities and worries about not living up to her own expectations or the expectations of others. Her fear becomes overwhelming and prevents her from even attempting to try out for the team. Zuri convinces herself that she would be ridiculed or rejected, leading her to avoid taking any risks. As a result, she misses out on an opportunity to pursue her passion and improve her soccer skills. To overcome this unhealthy side of fear, she needs to challenge her negative thoughts and beliefs. She can start by seeking support from friends or coaches who can provide encouragement and help her develop a growth mindset. By gradually exposing herself to challenging situations and reframing her fear, Zuri can learn to embrace failure as a steppingstone to success and unlock her full potential in soccer.

    Fear keeps you from doing the great things you are meant to do in life. What's in YOU? Think about the unique qualities that make you who you are. I rally behind you, pushing you to believe in yourselves, seek support, and never underestimate the impact you can have on the world once you overcome your deepest fears. I want to help you show up and shine!

Unleash Your S.H.I.N.E.

Shake what others have tried to make you out to be.

Heal yourself by embracing who you are.

Invite God into your space to inspire and ignite your creativity.

Notice what true colors others are showing you.

Encourage yourself to go after your hopes and dreams!

Self-Reflections for Shining: Illuminate Your Inner Self

1. What are some of my biggest fears or anxieties? How do they currently impact my life and decision-making?

   _____
   _____
   _____
   _____
   _____
   _____
   _____
   _____

2. How might the consequences of letting fear control my life limit my potential?

3. How can family, friends, or mentors assist me in facing my fears and provide encouragement along the way?

ABOUT THE AUTHOR

Sonya D. Nelson, a wife, mother, and educator, is an author with a passion to educate and empower the next generation. With her books, "Made 2 Shine: Embracing Who You Were Created to Be" and "Sparkle & Shine: Like Only YOU Can," she inspires and encourages others to embrace their true selves. Through her writings, she aims to start the conversations needed on our journey to fulfilling our purpose and being all we were created to be. With "Made 2 Shine" as her mantra, she serves, with a purpose, striving to make a positive impact and ignite the spark within others.

Made in the USA
Columbia, SC
01 December 2023